100 Things
You Really Need to Know
About Geography!

MW01488525

According to Bill Condon
Illustrated by Bettina Guthridge

CELEBRATION PRESS
Pearson Learning Group

GREEN LAN

ALASKA

CANADA

NORTH AMERICA

USA

MEXICO

BERMUDA TRIANGLE

CAN ISLA

EQUATOR

PACIFIC OCEAN

VENEZUELA

COLOMBIA

ECUADOR

SOUTH AMERICA

PERU

BOLIVIA

BRAZIL

CHILE

EASTER ISLAND

Atlases

1. First, you need an atlas,
   or a book of maps,
   so that you can explore
   the world and have just
   about the best fun you
   can have sitting down.

   (We couldn't fit all
   "100 Things" onto this
   map, but it's a start.)

2

Bargains

2. In 1867 the United States bought Alaska from Russia for $7.2 million. That was about 2 cents per acre.

3. A huge parcel of land, known as the Louisiana Territory, was bought by the United States from France in 1803. It was divided into 13 states, doubling the size of the United States. It cost $15 million, less than 3 cents an acre.

Capital Cities

4. Hungary's capital city, Budapest, received its name from two separate cities, Buda and Pest.

5. The capital of Singapore is Singapore.

6. Rome is the capital of Italy. According to legend, it was founded by Romulus and Remus, who were twin boys raised by a wolf.

7. In Caracas, Venezuela's capital, streets are blocked off on Christmas Eve so people can roller skate to church.

8. In 1928 the Olympic flame was first used in Amsterdam, the capital of the Netherlands.

Caves

9. Some caves in New Mexico
   are home to half a million bats.

10. New Zealand's Waitomo Caves
    have thousands of glowworm
    lights. (Glowworms are the
    larvae, or grubs, of tiny flies.)

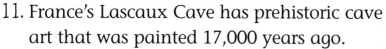

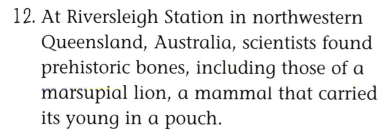

11. France's Lascaux Cave has prehistoric cave
    art that was painted 17,000 years ago.

12. At Riversleigh Station in northwestern
    Queensland, Australia, scientists found
    prehistoric bones, including those of a
    marsupial lion, a mammal that carried
    its young in a pouch.

Continents

13. The seven continents are Asia, Africa, North America, South America, Antarctica, Europe, and Australia.

14. Australia is the only country that takes up an entire continent. It is also the smallest continent.

Deserts

15. The Saharan sand sea of Isaouane-n-Tifernine, in Algeria, has the highest sand dunes in the world. Some of them rise to 1,526 feet.

16. The Mojave Desert, in Death Valley, California, has temperatures over 122° Fahrenheit.

17. In some parts of Africa's Sahara, hot desert air dries up raindrops before they reach the ground.

18. In Chile's Atacama Desert, it rained in 1971—for the first time in 400 years.

19. Antarctica is a desert, because rain hardly ever falls on it. However, it contains 70% of the world's fresh water, which has built up over thousands of years.

Earthquakes

20. Thousands of earthquakes occur every year.
    Most are so small we don't notice them.

21. The worst earthquake
    was in China in 1556.
    It killed about 830,000 people.

22. Fires and large, damaging waves
    called *tsunamis* often follow earthquakes.

Extremes

23. Earth's highest point is Mount Everest, on the border between Nepal and China.

24. Earth's lowest point is the Mariana Trench, in the Pacific Ocean.

25. The world's southernmost capital is Wellington, New Zealand.

26. The world's northernmost capital is Reykjavik, Iceland.

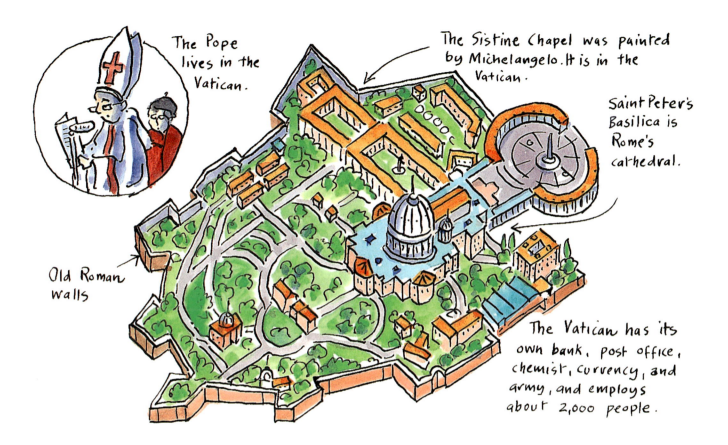

The Pope lives in the Vatican.

The Sistine Chapel was painted by Michelangelo. It is in the Vatican.

Saint Peter's Basilica is Rome's cathedral.

Old Roman walls

The Vatican has its own bank, post office, chemist, currency, and army, and employs about 2,000 people.

27. The smallest country in the world is the State of Vatican City, in the city of Rome, Italy. It has an area of about 0.27 square miles.

28. Greenland is the world's largest island.

29. Canada has the longest coastline (141,782.5 miles), and Monaco has the shortest coastline (3.47 miles).

30. Angel Falls in Venezuela is the world's highest waterfall. It has a total drop of 3,211 feet, which is more than twice the height of the Empire State Building.

Building is 381 m. or 1,250 ft. and TV mast brings it to 449 m. or 1,473 ft.

EMPIRE STATE BUILDING

31. At Hawaii's Mount Waialeale, it rains 350 days a year.

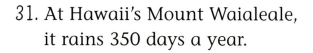

32. China has over 80,000 dams, the most in the world. Of these, 22,000 are categorized as large dams. They are as deep as, or deeper than, a four-story building.

33. Australia's Indian Pacific Railway line runs dead straight for 296 miles across the Nullabor Plain.

34. The 1980 eruption of Mount St. Helens, in the U.S. state of Washington, caused the world's biggest landslide.

35. Mandarin, a dialect of Chinese, is the most commonly spoken language in the world, followed by English.

Famous Structures

36. India's Taj Mahal was built as a tomb for the wife of an emperor. He wanted to ensure that she would always be remembered.

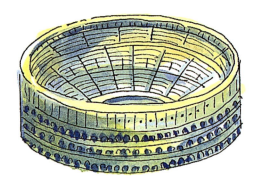

37. The Colosseum is where up to 50,000 ancient Romans watched battles that were fought between gladiators.

38. The Statue of Liberty's nose is 4.5 feet long. Each eye is 2.6 feet across.

39. The Eiffel Tower was built in Paris, France, in 1889. It was designed as a temporary tower, but it is still there today.

Geographic Giggles

40. Q What's furry and holds water?
A Hamsterdam (Amsterdam)

41. Q Where do sharks live?
A Finland

42. Q What do fish sleep on?
A A riverbed

43. Q What do rocks sit on?
A Rocking chairs

44. Q What's the tallest food tower in the world?
A The Leaning Tower of Pizza (Pisa)

Icebergs

45. Small, flat icebergs have been rigged with sails and navigated over thousands of miles.

46. Icebergs are made of fresh water.

47. A collision with a huge iceberg in the North Atlantic caused the sinking of the "unsinkable" RMS *Titanic* in 1912.

Islands

48. The Canary Islands are in the Atlantic Ocean, near the northwest coast of Africa. The islands were named by the ancient Romans, who had found wild dogs there. *Canis* is Latin for "dog".

49. There are about 30,000 islands in the Pacific Ocean.

Lakes

50. The Caspian Sea is actually the world's largest lake.

51. Lake Eyre is Australia's largest lake, but usually it doesn't have any water in it.

52. The Dead Sea is one of the world's saltiest lakes. It is nine times saltier than the oceans. People cannot sink in it because the salt keeps them afloat.

Monsters

53. Bigfoot is said to look like a giant ape. Is Bigfoot real? If it is, it lives in the northwest regions of the United States and Canada.

54. The yeti or abominable snowman of the Himalayas is another apelike creature. Many footprints have been found, but no yeti, yet.

55. Scotland's Loch Ness monster is supposed to be huge—but still no one can find it!

Mountains

56. Some mountains on the equator (the hottest area on Earth) are permanently covered with snow and ice.

57. The tallest mountain range above sea level is Asia's Himalaya Mountains.

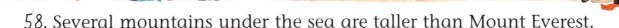

58. Several mountains under the sea are taller than Mount Everest.

59. The world's longest mountain range is the Mid-Atlantic Ridge, an underwater mountain range of the Atlantic Ocean. It extends from Iceland to Antarctica and is more than 40,000 miles long.

60. The Andes Mountain range, which stretches through seven South American countries, is the longest mountain range above sea level.

Natural Wonders

61. Before 1869, only a few people knew about the Grand Canyon in the United States. Now it attracts about five million tourists each year.

62. Australia's Great Barrier Reef is made from the skeletons of millions of tiny creatures called polyps, which are related to jellyfish. It is the longest reef in the world and can be seen from space.

Oceans

63. There are five oceans in the world—the Pacific, Atlantic, Indian, Southern (also called Antarctic), and Arctic. They all have one thing in common . . . salt water!

Odd Bits From All Over

64. Once explorers believed that if they sailed too far, they would fall off the edge of the world. They thought they would reach the horizon!

65. Even if you travel forever over land or sea, you can never reach the horizon.

66. Many ships and planes have disappeared in the part of the Atlantic Ocean called the Bermuda Triangle, southeast of the United States.

67. The geographic center of the United States is in Smith County, Kansas.

68. Like the outside of a loaf of bread, Earth's surface is called a crust.

Earth's crust

core

69. In some countries, such as New Zealand and the United States, you can find boiling mud pools.

70. El Dorado, in South America, was supposed to be a land with masses of gold. No one has ever found it.

71. The Night of the Radishes is held every year in Oaxaca, Mexico. Farmers carve figures from radishes and display them.

72. In Coober Pedy, South Australia, it is so hot that most people live in underground houses.

73. There are no roads, only canals, in the Italian city of Venice.

74. In South Africa, ostrich racing is a popular sport.

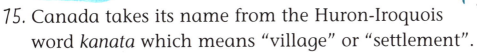

75. Canada takes its name from the Huron-Iroquois word *kanata* which means "village" or "settlement".

76. Mount Athos, in Greece, has a population of about 4,000 men. No women are allowed, and even female animals are banned.

77. If you flew from Tokyo, Japan, to Anchorage, Alaska, on Monday, you would cross the International Date Line and arrive on Sunday—the day before you left!

78. The equator passes through 13 countries: Ecuador, Colombia, Brazil, Saõ Tomé and Príncipe, Gabon, Republic of the Congo, Democratic Republic of the Congo, Uganda, Kenya, Somalia, Maldives, Indonesia, and Kiribati.

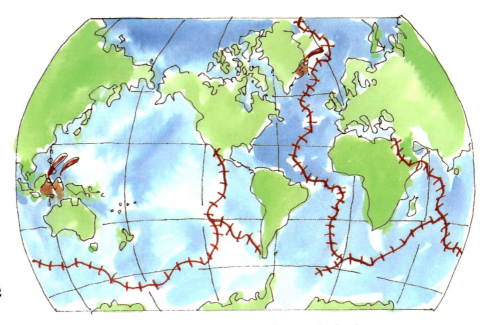

Plate Theory One

79. Scientists believe that Earth is divided into a number of shifting slabs, or plates. Most of the Earth's active volcanoes are found along these plates.

Plate Theory Two

80. Children believe that there's no point in washing plates, because they only get dirty again.

Pyramids

81. Egypt's three pyramids at Giza, just outside Cairo, were built as tombs for pharaohs.

82. The largest pyramid, built by Pharoah Khufu, at Giza, is made of more than 2 million blocks; the average weight of each is 2.5 tons.

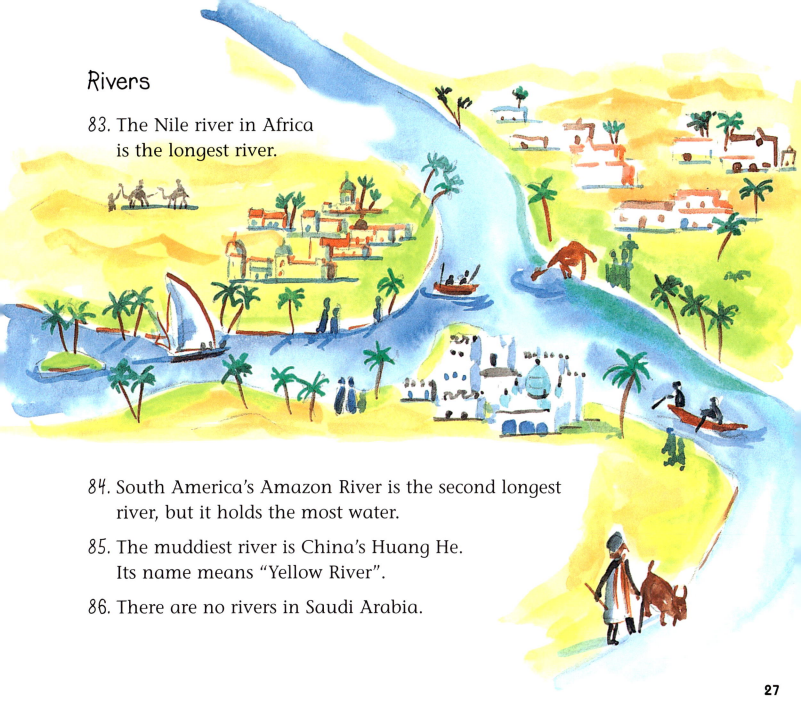

Rivers

83. The Nile river in Africa
    is the longest river.

84. South America's Amazon River is the second longest
    river, but it holds the most water.

85. The muddiest river is China's Huang He.
    Its name means "Yellow River".

86. There are no rivers in Saudi Arabia.

Rocks

87. Stonehenge, in England, is an ancient stone circle. No one knows exactly who erected it, or why.

88. Western Australia's 49-feet high Wave Rock curves over like a giant wave.

89. Large volcanic basalt columns make up the Giant's Causeway, in Northern Ireland. They look like stepping stones used by giants.

90. Australia's Uluru is the world's biggest monolith (rock).

91. Easter Island in the South Pacific is famous for its mysterious giant stone heads.

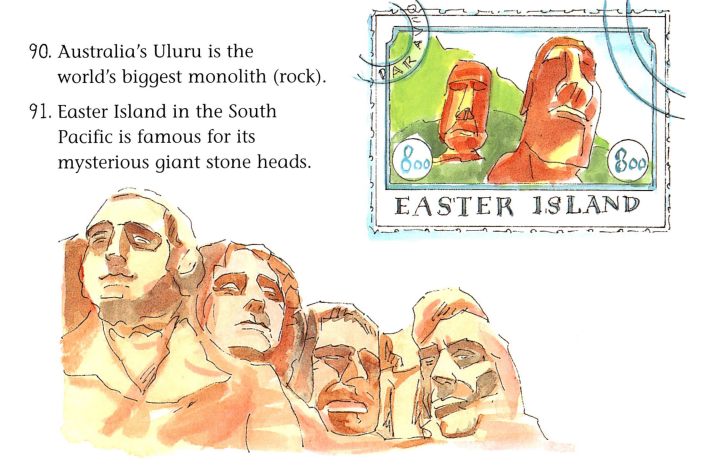

92. The faces of four United States presidents have been carved on Mount Rushmore, in South Dakota. They are George Washington, Thomas Jefferson, Theodore Roosevelt, and Abraham Lincoln.

Strange Names

93. These are all real names of United States towns: Santa Claus, Kickapoo, Surprise, Robinhood, Accident, Boring, Embarrass, Peculiar, and Whynot.

94. In France, there is a town named Y, and in Sweden there is a town named A.

Tidal Waves and Tsunamis

95. Destructive waves that crash on shore are often called tidal waves, but tidal waves are actually the crest of tides moving around Earth.

The highest tidal wave on record hit Japan in 1971. It was 85 m. or 278 ft. high — almost as high as New York's Statue of Liberty.

96. A *tsunami*—a Japanese word meaning "harbor wave" —can be caused by several things, including underwater earthquakes, volcanic eruptions, or landslides beneath the ocean surface.

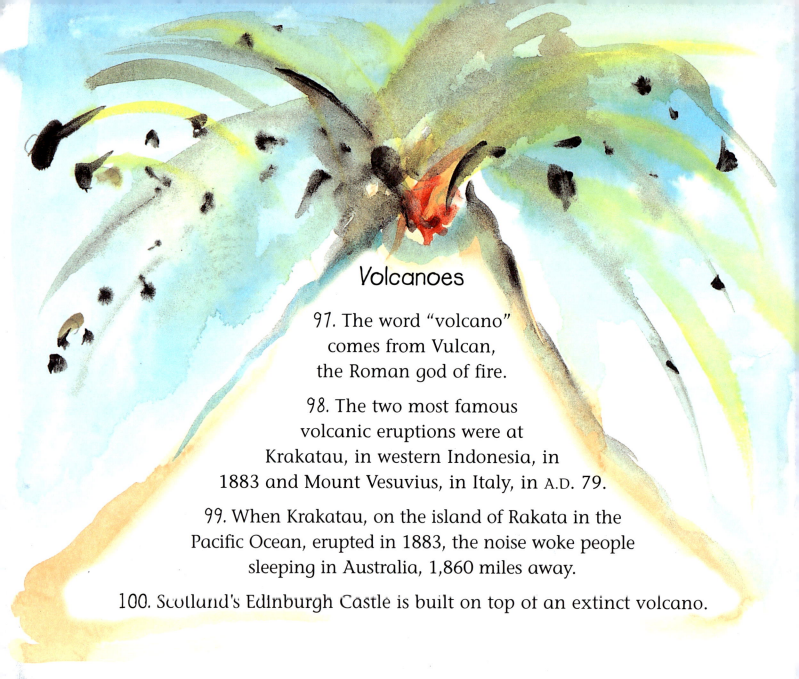

Volcanoes

97. The word "volcano"
comes from Vulcan,
the Roman god of fire.

98. The two most famous
volcanic eruptions were at
Krakatau, in western Indonesia, in
1883 and Mount Vesuvius, in Italy, in A.D. 79.

99. When Krakatau, on the island of Rakata in the
Pacific Ocean, erupted in 1883, the noise woke people
sleeping in Australia, 1,860 miles away.

100. Scotland's Edinburgh Castle is built on top of an extinct volcano.